Pg. 22

P9-DVK-923

Biofuels

David and Patricia Armentrout

Rourke
Publishing LLC
Vero Beach, Florida 32964

www.rourkepublishing.com

PHOTO CREDITS: © Olga Axyutina: Title Page; © Julie Fisher: Header; © Christian J. Stewart: page 4; © Bonnie Jacobs: page 5 top left; © Bjorn Kindler: page 5 top right; © Yenwen Lu: page 5 bottom; © Matthew Porter: page 7 right; © Magnus Johansson: page 7 top right; © luchschen: page 7; © Mark Smith: page 10; © Lilac Mountain: page 11; © Sai Yeung Chan: page 13; © Leon Bonaventura, © Andrey Prokhorov: page 13 inset; © Ronald Sherwood: page 14; © kngkyle2: page 15; © PhotoDisc: page 17 top; © Mark van Vuren: page 17 bottom; © Samuel Acosta: page 19; © Amanda Rohde: page 20; © AVTG: page 21, 43; © Heiko Potthoff: page 22 left; © Peter Garbet: page 22 right; © Slaw Omir Fajer: page 23; © Sandra Caldwell: page 26 right; © dgmata: page 26 left; © Sandra Day: page 27 top right, 31; © Vartanov Anatoly: page 27 left; © General Motors Photo/Jeffery Sauger: page 27 top right; © AM29: page 28; Courtesy: Library of Congress: page 29 top; © Christophe Testi: 29 bottom; © Ben McLeish: page 32; © ArtEfficient: page 33; © Andrew Dernie: page 34; Courtesy: Sandia/Photo by Randy Wong: page 35; © Mona Makela: page 36, 37; © Mark Strozier: page 39; Courtesy: Oregon State University: page 39 inset; © Ralph125: page 40; © Claudia DeWald: page 41; © Leif Norman: page 43 inset; © Laurence Gough: page 44, 45

Edited by Kelli L. Hicks

Cover design by Nicky Stratford, bdpublishing.com
Interior design by Teri Intzegian

Library of Congress Cataloging-in-Publication Data

Armentrout, David, 1962-
  Biofuels / David and Patricia Armentrout.
     p. cm. -- (Let's explore global energy)
  ISBN 978-1-60472-321-2
  1. Biomass energy--Juvenile literature. I. Armentrout, Patricia, 1960- II. Title.
  TP339.A76 2009

  662'.88--dc22

                    2008025133

Printed in the USA

CG/CG

Rourke Publishing

www.rourkepublishing.com – rourke@rourkepublishing.com
Post Office Box 3328, Vero Beach, FL 32964

Table of Contents

CHAPTER ONE

Energy

We all use it. In fact, we use it every day. It powers our machines, heats our buildings, and lights our homes. Without it, transportation in our modern world would be nearly impossible. What is it? You probably already guessed that it is energy. Energy powers our lives. Energy is the ability to do work, and we use it to produce everything we have.

Finding enough energy to meet the demands of an energy hungry world is one of the biggest challenges facing us today.

People, plants, and animals have something in common. All need energy to survive. Where does energy come from? Energy comes from many sources. Plants, for example, collect light energy from the Sun and make their own food. Animals get energy from the food they eat. Animals convert the energy stored in food into energy they can use.

Of course, we get energy from food, too. Food keeps our bodies moving, but we also use energy in other ways. We convert some forms of energy into fuels to make our lives easier and more comfortable. Some of these fuels are biofuels. Biofuels are mostly plant-based fuels. Biofuels may one day replace **petroleum** products, like gasoline, as the main source of fuel for cars and trucks.

CHAPTER TWO

Energy Sources

Renewable Energy

SOLAR ENERGY

- Heat and light energy from the Sun
- Renews day after day as the Sun shines

WIND ENERGY

- Motion energy from the wind
- Renews day after day as the wind blows

HYDROPOWER ENERGY

- Energy from moving water
- Renews day after day in waves and flowing rivers

GEOTHERMAL ENERGY

- Heat and steam energy beneath the Earth's surface

BIOMASS ENERGY

- Plant material and animal waste used to generate energy

According to the U.S. Energy Information Administration, nonrenewable energy sources, including fossil fuels and nuclear power, provide more than 92 percent of the world's energy needs. Renewable energy sources contribute just over seven percent.

Nonrenewable Energy

COAL

- Solid that takes millions of years to form
- Mined from the Earth

OIL

- Liquid that takes millions of years to form
- Pumped from the ground

NATURAL GAS

- Colorless odorless gas that takes millions of years to form
- Pumped from the ground

PROPANE GAS

- Natural gas that becomes a liquid gas at high pressure or at low temperature
- Found with natural gas and oil

NUCLEAR ENERGY

- Stored in atoms-the smallest particles of chemical elements
- Formed using uranium ore which is mined from the earth

CHAPTER THREE

Renewable vs Nonrenewable

Biomass is plant material used to make biofuels and to produce biopower. Therefore, biofuels are renewable. Renewable energies like biofuel, solar power, and wind power, are important to our future because they don't run out. Natural forces constantly renew, or replenish them.

While we do use renewable energy in some places, most of our energy comes from a nonrenewable source, fossil fuels. We burn fossil fuels, including coal, oil, and natural gas, for energy.

Fuel for Thought

About 86 percent of the world's energy needs come from fossil fuels.

CHAPTER FOUR

The Problem with Fossil Fuels

The world depends on fossil fuels. Inexpensive fossil fuels have improved the quality of life for many people. Try to imagine what life might be like without gasoline to power our vehicles, or coal to produce electricity. So, what's the problem? Let's begin with pollution.

Fossil fuels take a toll on the environment. They cause obvious problems such as oil spills and smog filled air. They also cause other, more complicated problems that are not so easy to see. **Acid rain**, for example, caused partially by sulfur in fossil fuels, damages buildings and harms trees, aquatic life, and insects.

Pollution mixes with clouds and forms acid rain.

13

Fuel for Thought

Carbon dioxide is a colorless odorless greenhouse gas. Most of the carbon dioxide in our atmosphere comes from forest fires, volcanic eruptions, and from burning fossil fuels.

Some scientists also blame **global warming** on our use of fossil fuels. Global warming is the increase in the average temperature of the Earth's atmosphere caused by **greenhouse gases**. Some greenhouse gases occur naturally, but we release more into the atmosphere when we burn fossil fuels.

Greenhouse gases act as a blanket around the Earth. They trap heat and warm the planet. Without the blanket, Earth would be cold and uninhabitable. But, if the blanket gets too heavy, the planet could warm too much.

Scientists are concerned that global warming will change Earth's climate and weather patterns. Warmer temperatures could also melt massive ice sheets, raising sea levels around the world. Rising seas would flood low-lying coastal areas displacing millions of people.

Do fossil fuels cause global warming? We don't know for sure, but scientists around the world are busy trying to find out.

Some solar radiation is reflected by the Earth and the atmosphere.

Some of the infrared radiation passes through the atmosphere, and some is absorbed and re-emitted in all directions by greenhouse gas molecules. The effect of this is to warm the Earth's surface and the lower atmosphere.

Some radiation passes through the clear atmosphere.

Most radiation is absorbed by the Earth's surface and warms it.

Infrared radiation is emitted from the Earth's surface.

CHAPTER FIVE

Back to the Future

There is another problem with fossil fuels. Remember, they are a nonrenewable energy source. Experts say the world's fossil fuel supplies are dwindling. They could be gone within the next 50 to 100 years, maybe sooner. Where will our energy come from then?

If fossil fuels are an energy source soon to be in our past, then biofuels may be the fuels of the future. Biofuels, however, are by no means new; people have used them for thousands of years.

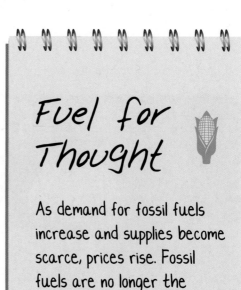

Fuel for Thought

As demand for fossil fuels increase and supplies become scarce, prices rise. Fossil fuels are no longer the bargain they once were.

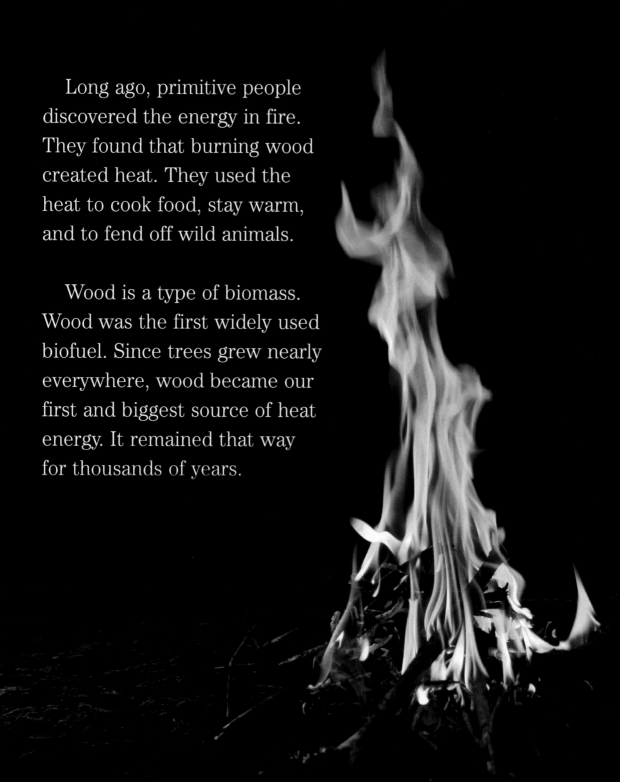

Long ago, primitive people discovered the energy in fire. They found that burning wood created heat. They used the heat to cook food, stay warm, and to fend off wild animals.

Wood is a type of biomass. Wood was the first widely used biofuel. Since trees grew nearly everywhere, wood became our first and biggest source of heat energy. It remained that way for thousands of years.

Fuel for Thought

In the United States, wood is no longer a major source of
biomass fuel. According to the U.S. Energy Information
Administration, wood provides only about two percent of
America's energy needs.

CHAPTER SIX

Biomass

Using biomass as fuel seems like a good idea because there are so many sources of raw materials. Biomass comes from animals, plants, and even trash. It includes manure from livestock, trees, grass clippings, and crops. Major biomass crops include corn, sugarcane, soybeans, and sugar beets. Some biomass, like wood, is burned directly. Some is processed into biofuels. Either way, we use biomass because it has stored energy. But, where does the energy in biomass come from? It all starts with plants and **photosynthesis**.

CHAPTER SEVEN

The Power of Photosynthesis

Most of the energy we use is a result of photosynthesis; the process plants use to make food. During photosynthesis, plants use **chlorophyll**, a green pigment, to capture light energy from the Sun. The energy helps plants change water and carbon dioxide into **glucose**. Plants use glucose, a simple sugar, as food, or they convert the sugar to a starch and store it for later use.

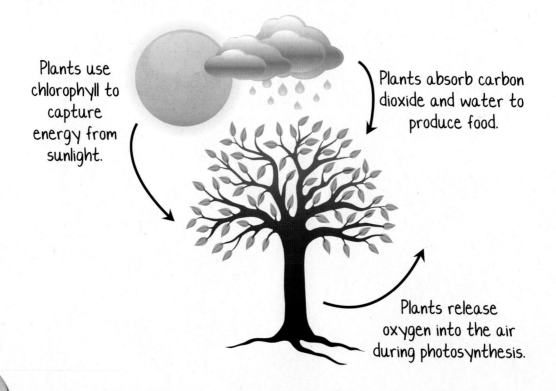

Plants use chlorophyll to capture energy from sunlight.

Plants absorb carbon dioxide and water to produce food.

Plants release oxygen into the air during photosynthesis.

The Carbon Cycle

Carbon is the fourth most abundant element in the universe. It is a building block of all living things and is found nearly everywhere on Earth. Carbon exists in fossil fuels, soil, water, plants, and animals, and in our atmosphere as carbon dioxide gas. We release carbon dioxide gas when we burn fossil fuels and biomass. In turn, plants absorb some of the gas during photosynthesis. Carbon constantly moves in a cycle and never goes away. The carbon cycle is nature's way of moving carbon where it's needed.

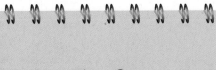

Fuel for Thought

Plants help clean the air by absorbing carbon dioxide and releasing oxygen.

ELEMENT	PART PER MILLION
Hydrogen	739,000
Helium	290,000
Oxygen	10,700
Carbon	4,600
Neon	1,340
Iron	1,090

CHAPTER EIGHT

Biofuels

Fossil fuels and biofuels are similar in one important way. The energy locked within them is the result of photosynthesis. Because the energy in fossil fuels and biofuels comes from the Sun, you could say they are both a form of solar energy.

Fossil fuels formed from the remains of plants and animals, which lived millions of years ago (ancient biomass). Those plants and animals stored energy in their cells. We release that energy when we burn fossil fuels. Biomass has stored energy too. Biofuel processing plants convert that energy into oil and alcohol fuels we use today.

 VS

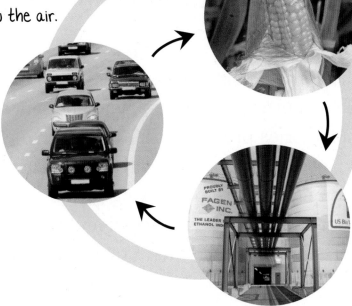

Plants absorb cabon dioxide from the atmosphere for photosynthesis.

Ethanol is burned as fuel, which releases carbon dioxide into the air.

Ethanol factories use plants to make ethanol.

Fuel for Thought

Animals benefit from photosynthesis too. Since animals cannot make their own food, they eat plants, or other animals that eat plants. Animals get their energy from the sugars and starches in plants.

CHAPTER NINE

Ethanol Fuel

Ethanol is an alcohol fuel made from the sugars found in plants. It is flammable and produces heat energy when burned. Ethanol factories produce ethanol from many types of biomass, especially corn and sugarcane. Farmers grow the biomass and sell it to processing plants. Processors convert the biomass to ethanol and sell it, mostly for use as a motor vehicle fuel. Ethanol is a common type of biofuel because it is easy to make.

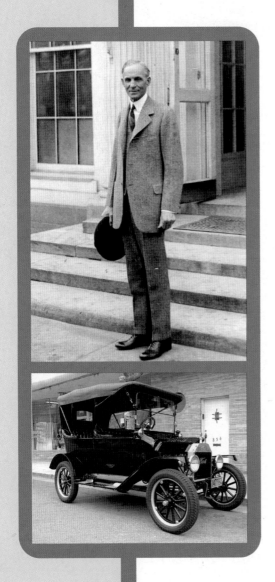

Fuel for Thought

Henry Ford was an American inventor and founder of the Ford Motor Company. In 1908, his company introduced the Ford Model T automobile. The Model T, built to run on gasoline or ethanol, was the first mass-produced car in the world. Ford supported the use of ethanol fuel over gasoline. Ethanol, he reasoned, would help American farmers who grew the crops to make the fuel. Gasoline, however, was cheaper than ethanol and soon became the fuel of choice for carmakers and consumers. Henry Ford once said that he believed ethanol was the fuel of the future. Maybe he was right.

CHAPTER TEN

Corn Ethanol

Corn is the largest **agricultural** crop in the United States. Farmers grow it to feed livestock and for human consumption. Increasingly, farmers are also growing corn to supply the U.S. ethanol **industry** with raw biomass.

Ethanol factories add **enzymes** to giant tanks of corn. The enzymes help convert corn sugars into alcohol in a process called fermentation. The finished product, ethanol, is added to gasoline to make gasohol. Gasohol is a blend of 90 percent gasoline and 10 percent ethanol. Also known as E10, gasohol is available at gas stations around the U.S. Most car engines burn gasohol as easily as they burn gasoline.

Fuel for Thought

Some experts are concerned that farmers will not be able to grow enough corn to satisfy our need for both food and fuel.

CHAPTER ELEVEN

Sugarcane Ethanol

Some forms of biomass are better ethanol producers than corn. Brazil, for example, uses sugarcane. Experts point out that an acre of sugarcane produces about 700 gallons of ethanol, while an acre of corn produces only 350 gallons.

In an effort to reduce their dependence on foreign oil, Brazil requires that all motor vehicle fuels contain a blend of at least 24 percent ethanol. Brazil's use of ethanol has greatly reduced the amount of petroleum they import.

Sugarcane is cut and taken to be processed.

CHAPTER TWELVE

Energy Crops

Many scientists believe the best strategy for producing ethanol from biomass is to use energy crops rather than food crops. Energy crops include fast growing trees like poplar and native grasses like switchgrass. Energy crops require less fertilizer and are more productive. Energy crops, grown on farms just like food crops, are better for the environment and cost less to produce.

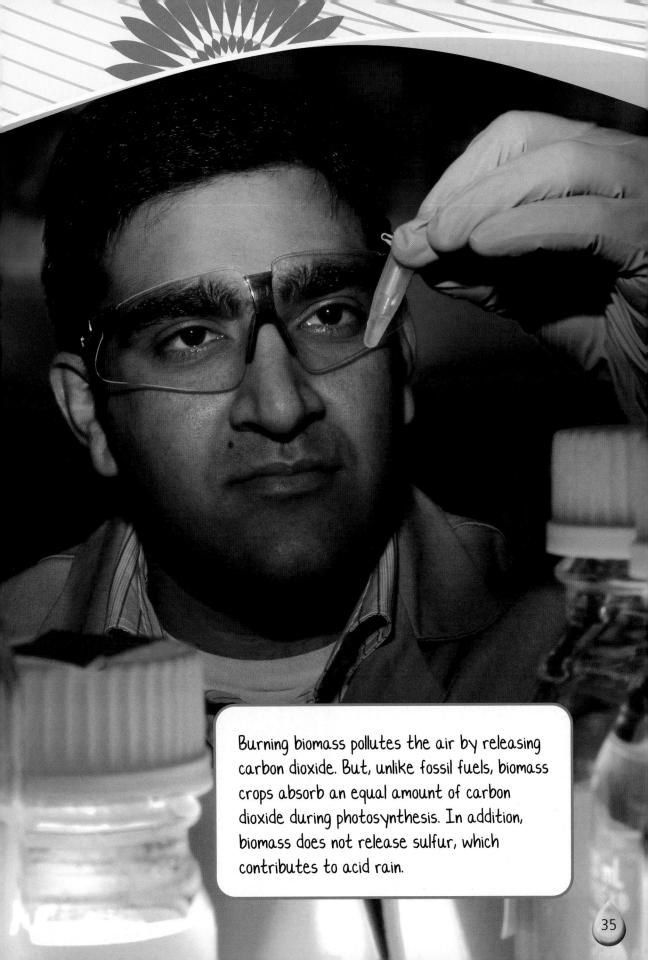

Burning biomass pollutes the air by releasing carbon dioxide. But, unlike fossil fuels, biomass crops absorb an equal amount of carbon dioxide during photosynthesis. In addition, biomass does not release sulfur, which contributes to acid rain.

CHAPTER THIRTEEN

Biodiesel

Big vehicles like trucks, buses, boats, and construction equipment typically have diesel engines. Diesel engines run on diesel fuel processed from crude oil, a fossil fuel. Biodiesel is a fuel for diesel engines made from vegetable oil or animal fats. Soybean oil and canola oil are two vegetable oils used to make biodiesel.

Using biodiesel has many advantages over using petroleum diesel. For one, it is plant-based, therefore a renewable energy.

Secondly, biodiesel lubricates moving engine parts better than petroleum diesel, so it reduces wear and tear on engines. Also, biodiesel exhaust does not smell bad (some say it smells like popcorn!) or release harmful **emissions** that contribute to acid rain.

HYDROGEN & VEGGIE OIL POWERED

Fuel for Thought

It takes less energy to make biodiesel from plant oils than it takes to distill corn for ethanol.

Some scientists are excited about the potential of **algae** as a source of biodiesel. Algae are oily plants that grow quickly. If grown in the right conditions, algae can double in size in just hours. Algae can also be harvested every day.

Algae production is expensive. However, oil companies, universities, and the National Renewable Energy Laboratory are experimenting with algae. They hope to find an **efficient** way to grow it. Algae could one day become a major source of biomass.

Fuel for Thought

Scientists believe algae could produce up to 5,000 gallons of biofuel per acre!

CHAPTER FOURTEEN

Biogas

Biogas is gas released when **organic** matter, such as plant biomass, animal waste, and landfill waste, breaks down.

Methane is a powerful biogas that forms in landfills. It slowly builds as waste decays under soil and pressure. Methane from landfills is highly flammable, clean burning, and renewable. Power plants use methane to produce electricity. Methane biogas is also a valuable cooking and heating fuel.

Fuel for Thought

Can elephant waste be our new big supply of biogas? Maybe, elephants and other zoo animals already provide biomass. The Dallas Zoo has a plan to turn animal manure and yard waste into power. Instead of paying to have animal waste removed, the zoo will use it to produce biogas. The biogas will power a generator to produce electricity for the zoo.

CHAPTER FIFTEEN

Biopower

Biopower is another way to use energy from biomass. Biopower plants generate electricity by burning biomass. They work much like fossil fuel power plants. The biggest difference is the fuel. Biopower plants burn agricultural and forestry waste as well as scrap from industry.

Most power plants burn fuel in giant furnaces. The furnaces boil water, which turns to steam. The steam spins a **turbine**. The turbine rotates a magnet around a coil of wire generating electricity.

Forestry waste is collected
and burned as Biofuel.

CHAPTER SIXTEEN

The Energy Puzzle

Can we solve the energy puzzle before it's too late? Bright minds and hard working people are trying to put the pieces together. Biofuels and other renewable energies seem to offer hope for an energy hungry world, but experts will first have to overcome many challenges.

Someday soon, a motivated scientist will find the missing piece to the world's energy puzzle. Maybe it will be you!

Glossary

acid rain (ASS-id-RAYN): polluted rain from gas released from burning fossil fuels

agricultural (AG-ruh-KUL-chur): business of producing crops and raising animals

algae (AL-jee): small plants that grow in water or damp areas

carbon dioxide (kar-buhn dye-OK side): colorless, odorless gas

chlorophyll (KLOR-uh-fil): green pigment in plants

efficient (uh-FISH-uhnt): work without wasting energy

emissions (I-MISH-uhnz): harmful chemicals released into the air

enzymes (EN-zimz): proteins that cause a chemical reaction

greenhouse gas (GREEN-houss-GAS): gas trapped in the atmosphere

global warming (GLOH-buhl-WAHR-ming): rise in the Earth's air and water temperatures caused by greenhouse gases

glucose (GLOO-kose): plant sugar

industry (IN-dus-tree): manufacturing companies and other business

organic (or-GAN-ik): of biologic origin

petroleum (puh-TROH-lee-uhm): oil or crude oil

photosynthesis (FOE-toe-SIN-thuh-siss): a chemical process by which plants make their food

turbine (TUR-bine): an engine driven by air, water, steam, or gas

Index

Further Reading

Solway, Andrew. *Biofuels.* Gareth Stevens Publishing, 2007.

Storad, Conrad J. *Fossil Fuels.* Lerner Publications, 2007.

Wheeler, Jill. *Renewable Fuels.* ABDO Publishing, 2007.

Websites to Visit

www.eia.doe.gov/kids/energyfacts

http://science.howstuffworks.com/energy-channel

http://powerhousekids.com

About the Authors

David and Patricia Armentrout specialize in nonfiction children's books. They enjoy exploring different topics and have written about many subjects, including sports, animals, history, and people. David and Patricia love to spend their free time outdoors with their two boys and dog Max.